ITEMS IN THE NEWS

Praise for *180 Days: Reflections and Observations of a Teacher*

"This beautiful book of poems, *180 Days: Reflections and Observations of a Teacher*, is a magnificent celebration of the educational process and the creative process in the practice of poetry."

— Dr. Alla Bozarth, Episcopal Priest,
Wisdom House, Sandy, Oregon

"Do yourself a favor and read this wonderful and profoundly moving book. . . . Over my forty-year career in education, I have enjoyed reading numerous fine books written by teachers about their students and their work. This book is unlike any I have read before. It cannot be stereotyped and is decidedly not 'cute,' 'charming,' or 'blaming.' It is instead a deeply affecting tribute to great teaching and complex learners, presented as the thoughtful and hope-filled insights of a phenomenal educator and as the poetic responses of his inspired students."

— Dr. Trudi Taylor, Professor Emerita,
University of St. Thomas

"Every section in *180 Days: Reflections and Observations of a Teacher*, indeed every poem, moved me deeply. Here is a book whose reflections on teaching is truly a work of art, one that should be read by teachers and parents, past, present and future."

— Carolyn Holbrook, Composition and Creative
Writing Instructor at Hamline University,
2010 recipient of the Minnesota Book
Awards' Kay Sexton Award

ITEMS IN THE NEWS

STAN KUSUNOKI

NORTH STAR PRESS OF ST. CLOUD, INC.
St. Cloud, Minnesota

Published by
        North Star Press
        19485 Estes Road
        Clearwater, MN 55320
        www.northstarpress.com

Section C:
Weather, Outdoors, and Personals

Personals

Section A:

Histories, International and
National Stories, Editorials

The 49 Bus . . .

. . . rolls out from Mission and up Van Ness
Neighborhood changes marked by beer billboards:
First, Tecate
then Tsingdao
then Kirin, Bud Light
Fat woman fumbles in her bra pocket
Breasts dancing a jig
as she searches for her bus pass
Barrio boys hip their way past her
and the wide-eyed Chinese girl,
flashing teeth and coyote eyes
Tourists ask the bus driver
for the way to Haight

I get off at Sutter Street
Where the sign reads Japanese,
but says "se habla Español"
Right here, in this block, gramps made suits and dresses
stitching together his American dream
Which storefront displayed his handiwork?
Maybe 1214, across from Osaka Grill
Under iron balcony and over plywood vestibule
the sign, pink lettered with heels
says "Foot Worship"

I like the thought of it
The shop descending from garments for the body
to coverings for the feet

Egret-legged Latinas walk by smelling of gardenias
I stifle a sneeze but savor the moment
imagining them in full-skirted Kusu Custom Tailor
Swirling toward evening

Imagining grandfather reveling
in this particular angle of sunlight
on apartment walls, and wondering
if that memory turned him to painting
when he was taken from his shop
to barracks of dust and sand

Did he walk down the hill to Taylor Street
tracing a spirit path I now follow?
And what would he think to see me
on the ninth floor of the Hilton
writing his city, his street?
Or, did he only turn uphill
back across Van Ness
to Nihonmatchi—Japantown—
never crossing the boundary
where the signs change?

Journeys
(for Morinobu Kusunoki)

1. (1987)
You are here under my feet, these potted plants
flowers soon to wither. A husk of you
hermetically sealed and shrink wrapped
your funeral, the final attempt at preserving life

This is where we come and remember
A signpost, the etched letters
Solid, hard on our fingers
"This is real," we say, standing
on the immaculate lawn
trying to conjure you
You are not here

2. (1911)
I see you other places:
A boat, large, imposing
you, young, scared, excited
A new world awaits you
A promise
I pass you going west
across the Pacific
I know where you end
I search for beginnings

3. (1987)
A frustration!
You are not here
Not among the neon hustle-bustle
McDonalds, billions sold
I jostle through crowds
Tokyo, your city,

but not this place,
this modern megalopolis
I walk away
Cross rivers, catch a scent
A pebble you carried with you
as you met your future wife
in her father's clockworks
is all I find
I rub its glassy cool surface
It releases fragments only, of your memory
A girl, a pocket watch, tears,
You saying, "I will come back
Come back and take you to this place
where dreams can be made by hand."
The clock factory is gone
I put the pebble in my pocket
It holds the day's warmth

4. (1925, 1942)

A glimpse of you coming and going
Up and across Sutter Street
Packages arrive, and women appear
in dresses and coats, your handiwork
The shop is not here, though
It may as well have been bombed
in the war. As if Kamikaze had turned
on you, blowing your dreams to splinters
Strangers are here now
You did not return

5. (1987, 1942)

Another marker, that's all
Stone pylon
All that remains of a dream gone awry
I do not see the stables, barbed wire

Searchlights, guard tower,
But you do
You pass by confused
Your wife, your daughter, two sons
Arms tired with furoshiki bundles
and suitcases holding bits
of collected dreams
Between countries—not what you envisioned
the new world to be
You sit in a chair, pencil and paper in hand
What do you see? New dreams
stitched—a patchwork cloak?
Or just mountain cold
dust and tumbleweeds?

6. (1958)

I see you best here
Not Chicago, not San Francisco
Not Topaz, not even
The suburbs of my teens
But here. The basement
Southside Minneapolis
Me, five or six coming in the side door
A moment of blindness
I smell mildew, machine oil
Hear the whirring in the corner
Your treadle Singer machine
And you bent over it like Geppetto
A new suitcoat in the making
It must be Easter, then
Such a wealthy childhood
Custom church clothes every spring
And a private art tutor to boot!
You look over your shoulders
Explain how you make paintings

Sketching first, then adding the barest
film of pigment—your brush
skating on melting ice
Back and forth, building, an elm tree
a finch, conjuring Lake Harriet
on watercolor paper

And then, you, garden mentor
Hands grubby from weeding
as we savor the crisp sweetness
of carrots just pulled

Fabric, watercolors, and dirt
Our soul's cement
made fast

7. (1986, 1987)

I don't like seeing you here
Your season of "can't"
Stranger, though people here
All speak Japanese, know the old stories
Sing the old songs—"Momotaro, the Peach Boy"
You look out at the L.A. sky changeless as tombstone
Receive guests with a nod, a listless wave
You are a faded home movie here
The light's not clear, the image flickers
Shadows thick, I leave just as quickly
as you did, returning to this plot
where I change the flowers
add some water
drive through the gates
my journeys extensions of your own

Cranes

I see two cranes, grandfather
Brushstrokes on paper
Transforming blank sheet
into form and energy
Lost dreams
into hope, new trajectories
Look how they rise against
the gray anxious mists
the mountains you painted
from the stoop of the barracks
that replaced the bustle of Taylor Street
with the dust of Topaz, Utah

The cranes rise upward
free in flight
Against the voices of "No"
Against fear and hatred
Against not knowing

In this painting
There are no guard towers
No searchlights
No barbed wire
To deny your spirit,
confine your soul
Fly on, and I will follow

How It Happened

Folks would say it happened
Because of the war
Because of Executive Order 9066
Because General John DeWitt
turned California, Oregon, Washington, and Arizona
into "Military Areas"
Because people were afraid
And we were the threat
In Japanese, there is a word for it:
"Shigatakanai"
"That's the way it is"
"Nothing to be done . . ."
Folks will say
"That's how it happened"

But then, how did it not happen?
The East Coast was not declared
A "Military Area"
Where U-boats lingered off-shore
how many Germans or Italians
boarded out of their own homes?
How many pulled from the rich earth
That nurtured the dreams of their parents?

Shigatakanai
It is the end result
but not the reason
It happened the first time
someone said, "yellow man," "coolie"
It happened the first time
a kid pulled the corners of his eyes
upwards in a squint, sing-songing
"Ching Chong, Chinaman"

It happened the first time
someone said, "send them back
for their own good"

How did it happen?
Shigatakanai
That's the way it is
Shigatakanai
And the way it will continue
Shigatakanai
Nothing to be done
Shigatakanai
Shit happens
Shigatakanai
Shigatakanai
Shigatakanai

In a Name

I am the only one in my family with my name
It has not been handed down by generations
I am nobody's namesake
I have a made-up name
It would give my ancestors fits
Su Ta Na Ri
as close as they could get
Mouths straining to produce
consonants in conjunction
Sounds that do not exist in their world

My name is a disguise
born out of fear
Mother cloaking in English tweeds
pulled fur of Shetland sheep
her cotton kimono boy
hoping to spare him from soldiers' gaze
that in days to come
might turn ugly again
and present barbed wire as a dream surrogate
just as her fragrant, rich loam
birthing strawberries and peaches
was replaced by dust and desert

I know I have a real name
Ghosts of ancestors have said so
It is somewhere in Southern California soil
Deep in nurturing earth
Beyond the reach of herbicides, fungicides
fertilizer and herbicides
Beyond the reach of unknown hakujin farmer's
plow and tiller
A seed carried across vast oceans
Waiting to spring roots
Pushing into sunlight a shoot
Blooming the whispered word
The divine wind that names me

Smithsonian Exhibit: "Toward a More Perfect Union"

1.

Oh, ma, oh, pa
So much you have not said!
I look at this child
Look at her eyes
It is a look you understand—
The unvoiced "why?"
Your friends, in the space of a day
Walk sideways glancing now
from across the street
saying new words:
"Dirty Jap"
"Yellow Peril"

2.

I look through those eyes
at strangers in uniform
pieces of paper, their authority
I look at loaded trucks
Loaded trains
Uncomprehending the irony
The "Enemy" so hated
Understands loaded trucks and trains
Understands barbed wire
Understands hysteria and fear

That also allows here
The uniformed stranger
That also allows here
Tarpaper barracks
That also allows here
Barbed wire fencing

That also allows here
Guard towers and searchlights

Those eyes see that the farm is somehow gone
Or that the tailor shop is far
far from the dust you share with someone
else's family's sounds and smells
and uneasy sleep

3.

This
All this is you
Voices speak on the video screen
It is your story told over and over
A hundred and ten thousand times
This dit of time and space
needs be recreated, for only pylons
and roadside plaques now mark
the place where uniformed men stole dreams
stole even nightmares
for if not by dreams, then by nightmares
you could define yourselves
It is why we walk through ghostly fabrications
Walking back through darkness
To recover the dream and mark the point
Where dream and nightmare separate

4.

Then, take those stone pylons and burn into them
The child's eyes you know so well
Those eyes long averted
And have them look now
Straight out at the world
To all who cross this space
Whatever you call it
Manzanar
Poston
Topaz
Tule Lake
Gila River
Jerome
Rohwer
Heart Mountain
Minidoka
Amache
And tell them
"Nevermore!"

TB Ward—A Life in Two

She is coughing, coughing, coughing
Coughing up bits of her American Dream
Spittle on the sheet hems
The hems of her hospital white gown
to be tidied by white-masked nurses
patrolling the sheeted hedgerow
of rusty steel-frame beds
far away from her farm fields
hot sun, tomatoes, and strawberries
a lifetime ago across
this vast sea of whiteness

This new life conceived
In Arizona winter bedclothes
Desert sand clinging like skin grafts
The seed planted by strangers' breath
in the queues for rice
the queues for water
the queues to use the "benjo"

She knows if she makes it
out of this pale white garden
her life will be half
The ghostly missing self, separated by white
The desert seed issuing forth
the rows and rows of pale, quaking hedges
that block dreams of return
to the rich black soil
the glistening emerald fields
scarlet berries, voluptuous tomatoes
of the world before all color disappeared

The Shadowgraph Speaks

I am the remains of some
body once human
Once alive, just as you are
Living, hoping
I am now shadow
etched on rubble
a reminder of the devil
unloosed by your country
But not reminder enough
Your leaders use the same logic now
big talk and little thought
Their gentle voices oh so reasonable
Speaking in everyday tones the unspeakable

Listen!
You have not seen what I have seen
Felt what I have felt
Your movies, your television
even books cannot translate the horror

Can you imagine?
Your body burned, consumed to nothing
Not even ashes to be carried
to hallowed ground
no resting place, the final desecration

I am lucky
I have this remnant wall
my tombstone
But oh that my shadow would be burned
into the minds of all people
so you could not turn your faces
hide your conscience
cover your eyes

Look!
I am no longer human
but you are
If you speak the unspeakable,
then tell the truth
in the voices of the maimed and dying
in the emptiness of those already dead
I have no need of companions
Look to yourselves
That the world itself
not become shadow

Garden: the Banlieue of Paris

The flannel man digs in the rainy loam
Next to the railway—a plot of optimism
where jonquils' pointy tongues already
lick mulch, test the frost's departure

The flannel man wakes promises with prayer
Here, heady lavender, there, burning celosia
He stops and studies his earthy canvas
Conjures the blossoms of late summer

A train rackets by an arm's length away
The flannel man pays no attention
He is rooted here. Arms hover like Birds of Paradise
against the gray pavement, the dulling pulse of quartz

The flannel man fills his eyes with rain,
his mouth with sunlight. He smiles
sweat and dirt, sweet nectar—his benediction
then turns knowing the resurrection begins

Bouquet Garni

The herbs dry on Madame Mourre's
garage-top terrace as we drink
sharp berry Tavel wine
Everything is red and yellow
The light antiques the air we move through
It is the color of remembering
It smells of October,
as if somewhere nearby a vintner
burns leaves and vine prunings
shrouds of grapes pooling
in Madame Mourre's spare tumblers

And so our talk takes on the color of the air
We breathe in and exhale our histories
Rosemary, chevre, garlic, and crusty bread

Lyn passes a bowl as the ratatouille simmers
Adding its vital vegetable memories
to the air and our musings
So that when dinner is done
The sky is the crowded dusk of stories
Pulling down stars
the Mistral will blow away in the night
leaving lingering, tantalizing, a dream
scented by les Herbes de Province

Airport

The Hare Krishna saffron robes
Have been replaced by a Jehovah's Witness
and he's having a field day—
this Korean from New Jersey
plane delayed, a captive audience
Many others too, waiting
with many babies and nothing to do
Japanese
Chinese
Korean
Vietnamese
He knows all the languages
And has brochures, "Full color, you keep
and share with friends, relatives,
share with everyone"
Handing them out to the growing crowd
like the only Girl Scout for miles around
and everyone hungry for cookies

Flight 103—Lockerbie

Who is this Allah
whose name you invoke
to darken the sky
cause the Scottish highlands
to flow crimson?
What God
has such low regard for life
that you treat it
even your own sons and daughters
as chits on a game board?
Does this Allah revel
in the wailing of mothers
the cries of the broken
the stares of the dead?
Or do you invoke his name
Just as "Christians" call on Jesus
to justify mayhem?
Cinders fall from the sky
They are tears that burn
The tears of Allah
The tears of God

Recruit

I guess I can understand
ISIS recruits
In Syria, Afghanistan
What other hope for a life?
What hope of anything at all
other than simmering in a doorstop
propaganda your truth
your daily prayers?

But here, in the land of opportunity?
Why would you give this up
for a debasement of the religion
your mother taught you so well?

Why would you give up
The lake paths
The parkways
The turn of the seasons
For desert dust, heat unrelenting?
Why?
Unless your hope of a life
Is the same as the teenager
In a Damascus doorstep
Simmering?

Chills

The part of me that is my mother
The one who is a teenager, Orange County
sharecropper's farm, trembles and shakes
with each news story of an "alleged"
Afghani, Arab, Muslim
Detained under murky suspicions—
"National security" the code for profiling
When the president talks of military tribunals
Or she hears so-called patriots talking trash
"They're not Americans, send 'em back
Back where they belong,"
the rubble winter of Kabul,
the red-washed streets of Mogudishu
A ghost shiver shakes her spine

Why she hesitates to wave the flag
She has seen it in her face
And behind the starry promise
the stripes of blood-won freedom,
she has seen the clenched fist, the gritted teeth
the firebomb eyes
She knows of winter in the desert
Olive-drab uniforms and carbines with the safety off
and home sweet home, blown or taken away
like yesterday's front page photos
fluttering, a broken-winged dove in the storm sewer grate
She shivers each time fingers point
Syrians, Somlalis
"Boat People" from Vietnam, Laos, Kampuchea
Honduras, and Haiti
The fenced-in Cubans
The Chicano deportees
The Chinese dude, unfortunate
Honda driver in Detroit

It's always some kind of "them"
"those people," "that kind"
Always, always, a neighbor pushed out the door
Their eyes locked in "why?"

She throws the deadbolt
Pulls the knitted Afghan of many colors
Close about her shivering shuddering frame

Not So Easy

Malena from just outside Chicago
doesn't miss school three days
into summer vacation
but misses Mrs. Aldrich
her third grade teacher
"Going into fourth grade," she says
"things are going to get lots harder."

If that were the only thing
to worry about,
I would be happy
in this time when childhood is lost
to music videos
commercials on TV, radio
gaming devices
the Internet
These bright young lights
dimmed down by mass culture
programming and big-box mentality

Do I worry about content
when a fifth grader announces
she prefers *The Hunger Games*
to E.B. White?
Not when third graders know how to "twerk"
And fourth graders can swear a blue streak
If you let them
And everyone it seems, compares notes
about who they are "going with"

Oh, yes, teaching is my job
But the subtext—while growing young minds
to also deter the forces
that give kids too much, too soon
Silly, goofy, and wide-eyed
Preferable in a ten-year-old
too jaded and oversexed
loaded down with big attitude
and big worries

Okay to be Malena from outside Chicago
Okay to worry that next year
Math is not going to be so easy
Okay to still have bright eyes
And no favorite book—
"Just all of them"
Okay to be Malena from just outside Chicago
Just for a few more years

"Imagine" Revisited
(thanks, John Lennon)
National Teacher Appreciation Week

Imagine
If every child had a teacher just like you
How much more prepared and confident
the world would be?

Imagine
If every child had a teacher just like you
How many guns and roadside bombs
Would be replaced by paintbrushes,
Saxophones,
Voices raised in many-part harmonies
Instead of raised in anger and distrust?

Imagine
If every child had a teacher just like you
How many heads of state
Would be chosen by knowledge
and critical thinking
instead of misinformation and fear?

Imagine
If every child had a teacher just like you
How many more fit bodies and sharp minds
Ready to do the heavy lifting
required in this new global market?

Imagine
If every child had a teacher just like you
How different the world would be
Then look and understand
What a difference you make
Every day with the children around you!

Terrorist?

California winter
Fifteen-year-old Syrian girl
walking to high school
living the dream
thinking Algebra II
variables slipping into place
one by one,
when passerby screams,
"Terrorist! Go back home!"

Home?
The two-bedroom flat
Converted Motel 6
off the trunk highway
shared with aunt and uncle
and their young family
where she studies late into the night
after putting siblings
and cousins to bed?
That home?

Or, the home she left
Crumbled concrete of Aleppo?
The fear of mortar rounds
and bullets

Just as the Pilgrims left
their cottages behind
Or the Irish abandoning
their potato fields
Or the Chechens
Or the South Vietnamese
Or the Hmong

Or the Mexicans, Chileans
Nicaraguans
The Jews

Should we send them all back, too?
Wave after wave of deportees
Until all that remains
Are Cherokee, Assiniboine
Anishinabe, Lakota
First Nations?

Really? Is this what you want?

Tell me
Who is the terrorist?
The girl who has visions—
Lab tech, doctor,
Helping her people
She now calls "American"
Or anonymous housewife
spewing dirt
from second-hand
dented–front fender Subaru?

Which one instills fear and loathing?
Which one shouting hatred
At the American Dream?

Canaries in the Mineshaft—2

They pick it up quickly
Focused through their own child lenses
the worry and outrage
of parents, grandparents,
aunts, and uncles

The day after election day
the children reflect a very
Un-United States
Seven-, eight-year-olds worry
about World War III
Latinos fret—
Relatives,
maybe even themselves
sent back to Mexico
And the girls in hijabs are
silent, eyes downcast

What do we as teachers
say to them?
What can allay their fears?
Can we pretend that anything
is normal now?

But we do, don't we?
Refocusing worries on music and art
Math and good books
Challenging them to look
not back to yesterday
But to tomorrow and tomorrow
Their time to shine

And so, in these canaries
With their candor and misgivings
we can find, and tap
into hope, understanding
and conspire with them
So they are not the bellwethers
in the mindshaft
but the evolution of new birds
Flying with their own wings
on the updraft of their own making

Walls

It didn't work in Berlin
Nor in Belfast
Walls do not contain
They do not keep out

Build tall
People will still climb over
Build wide
They will find ways around it
Build deep
They will still dig their tunnels

If you build a wall
You provide a magnet for defiance
Instead of deterrence
You feed the passion
and fervor
to break through
Make passage

If you build a wall
It becomes miles
Of billboard
A canvas for graffiti
And the art of protest

If you build a wall
You building for yourself
A sense of false security
That will blow up
Not along the border
But under your feet

Your own ancestors'
rage that you have forgotten
their hardship and pain
The work of their hands
and their hearts
The things that truly made
this country great

The Nativity in Aleppo

It is bleak midwinter—Syria
temperatures near freezing
but it is not snow falling
but bombs
Dark helicopters and MiG fighters
messengers of death
from a despot who would destroy
all who oppose his regime
A city laid waste

In the bleak midwinter
three curious orphans keep watch
from the cubic cave
that was their apartment
as White Helmets claw
through the rubble
of one more direct hit
hands frantic
as an arm is revealed
then a head
and after hours, a young widow
is pulled alive from the concrete tomb

In the bleak midwinter
The White Helmets'
sighs of relief turn to concern
The widow is heavy with child
Calls for a pallet
and a blanket
ring through the frosty air

In the bleak midwinter
here is a new tableau
In a grotto
that was once a school
No wandering star of wonder
but a solstice moon
A bruised and weary young woman
on a fold-out cot
No Seraphim and Cherumbim
but five White Helmets
hovering
No shepherds or wisemen
but three curious orphans
two stray dogs
and a feral cat wary
and watching in the shadows

In the bleak midwinter
there is a cry
not the wail of another uncle
who has lost a niece or nephew
to the deadly rain
but the cry of a baby
newborn
wrapped in tattered towels
and a torn nylon fiberfill parka
the gift of the three curious orphans

In the bleak midwinter
there are still miracles:
A brand-new girl
eyes wide, wide open
holding the future

Supreme Court Decision, 6/26/2015

Oh, how they wail
these "defenders of marriage"
like whites afraid of black folk
taking their hallowed dining counter
vinyl-clad stool
What are they afraid of?
Someone else gets their slice
of the wedding cake?
Or tax breaks
Or insurance coverage?

What are they defending?
All the heterosexual marriages
Gone bad?
Black eyes, black souls
Dead-beat dads
Or just plain dead
ex-wives?

How about abused and neglected
Children
Orphans of restraining orders
Or divorce
What about their clouded future
Their confused lives?

Do the "defenders of marriage"
Foster new beginnings?
Or close the closet door
and turn off the light,
too many mirrors and secrets
too close for comfort?

A Nod to Gil Scott Heron

The revolution that has been televised
and publicized and ballyhooed
is not the revolution
It is a death rattle
Give it your respects
and let it bluster itself into oblivion

The Real Revolution
will not need sound bites and photo ops
It will not need closed-door mumblings
in carcinogenic clouds
it will not need car bombs
plutonium
assault rifles

The Real Revolution
is quiet as a whispered
"I love you"
It is the Mexican farm laborer
marrying a Vietnamese restauranteur
and their child marrying the child
of an African-American teacher and Chinese reporter
and at the wedding
the Puerto Rican best man
falls in love with the second-generation
Hmong bridesmaid

When bebop first hit
The old guard didn't get it
Said, "What the hell is that Chinese music?"
Well dig this:

Chinese music IS jazz
Japanese music is rock 'n' roll
African music is opera
That is the real revolution
It is a myriad of earth tones
A glorious cacophony of song
It is a menu to mesmerize the taste buds
It is many languages understood
It is a children seeing other children
instead of stereotypes

So let the self-proclaimed revolutionaries
Stomp and bellow
And do not worry so much
It is the cry of the blue-suited Tyrannosaurus
Who has just realized the climate is changing

We are the revolution
We are the next step in the evolution
Of human beings
Being truly human

We are birds
Watch us fly!

The Adopted

You are not my mother
My mother died in Korea
You are not my father
though I don't know who,
I know you are not him
You bring me up in your image,
but look
My eyes are not your eyes
My skin not your skin
My heart, not your heart

When you brought me here, I wrote
my name on tiny scraps of paper
I wrote in Korean so I would not forget
and hid the scraps around the house
in books, behind vases, under your stereo
I know you have found some
I see your face uncomprehending
as you toss the fragment
a fragment of me
unthinking, in the trash
It's all right
I replace each one with five more
You call me "Kristy,"
but I know better
My name is all around me
under my feet
in the walls, the ceiling
It blows to me in my sleep
through heating ducts
and windowsills

You think I am your perfect
suburban daughter—
I get As and Bs
I am on the tennis team
I get asked to the prom
even though I am just a soph

You call me "Kristy"
but I know better
I know who I am
I am scraps of paper filling your house
covering your furniture
littering your yard
I am seven clean brushstrokes
You will not change me

Beyond Profiling

You can't call it profiling anymore
It is a learned reflex
Or worse yet, a bad habit
Police sees a young black man
Maybe a hood
Maybe slouching baggies
Hanging out
Maybe waiting for a pal
Maybe waiting for his mom
who is parking her Camry
down the block
Maybe just resting

Doesn't matter

Police sees trouble
Hand on the gun handle
even before he approaches
Oh, that police had
Superhuman eyes to see
There's no handgun tucked in the undies
No blade snugged by the ankle
Of that they had the mind reader's gift
Detecting intent
So every time
They would do the right thing

It's not just the police, either
It's the lone gunman in the movie house
The disillusioned teenager who sees terror
As the way to heaven
It's the Klansman burning crosses

It is anywhere, anytime anyone
Acts out of fear and hatred
Not using God's eyes
To see the humanity
The living beings
Seeing only the unnamed
Enemy, the evil empire
The other

So the real and only question
What will it take to see each other mirrored

The hopes for our children, and their children
The dreams of a life well-lived
That happiness that is peace
The wisdom that we are all
One species

Unique in this vast and
Unfathomable universe
That is God's eye?

God Gambles

The streets are pooled with God's tears
Mixed with innocent blood
And God wonders
"Have I done the right thing?
Creating this animal
Designed for reason, who acts out of fear?"
Fear creating a modern instinct
Hand to the gun handle
Quick with the trigger
But slow with compassion and understanding
Even as one of his own species
Hemorrhages within sight
Within reach

God wonders
"How to fix this?
Another flood? The slate
Again wiped clean?"
God looks at the many masses
Craning their eyes skyward
Mouthing "Why?"
And in that moment
God sends the spirit
Whatever you want to call it
Hoping for it to spark
A cleansing fire
That burns away fear
to reveal hope
Reducing walls to ashes
to reveal bridges
Vaporizing misunderstanding
to reveal grace

Then God sighs
Watching
Watching
The holy roll of the dice

Section B:

Local/Neighborhood Stories, Obituaries

Steve Loses His Day Job

Steve loses his day job
and that's a good thing
No more standing next
to the light rail maintenance
on Farmers' Market days
making minimum wage, if lucky

No more being drenched
because the new baseball stadium
took away his protective alcove
No more scowling mothers
as they hustle children
to the other side of the street

No more freezing in spring
or early fall the tattered
red polyfill parka, little
defense against any weather
No more worrying about where
to spend the night

No more. Thank you Section Eight
And those who would deny Steve
his roof and warm bed
are welcome to take his place
even for an hour, and remember
the implication in Jesus' words:
"That which you do NOT do
For the least of these . . .
You do not do for me."

Love Is the Law
(with thanks to Chan Poling and the Suburbs)

The Suburbs sing and it is so
Those who fear that marriage has been lessened somehow
are not hearing the words
seeing people dancing in the street
Not understanding
When you exclude some from the institution
it keeps the holy vows
from being truly
universal
and when you include all
then it is about love above all else

The true dangers to marriage
are not these dancers
Not the GLBT crowd
No, it is those who take vows on a whim
Letting peevishness and petty persuasions
Putting asunder what God has joined
Suburban swapping and urban whoring
more likely threats than two people
committed to each other
who just happen to be of the same sex

Look at the sea of happiness
Gay, straight, men, women
The palette of browns
from ivory to chestnut,
walnut to ombre
See septegenarians
their sons and daughters
hoisting another generation
upon their shoulders
to witness a dance of history

Oh, the children!
Understanding perhaps
only an excuse to jump and shake
and carry on with abandon
It is for them
we cheer and jive
Our hard work
So they may love and marry
because of love
Because love is the law at last

Items in the News

1.

Fear came into our neighborhood
Or rather, it showed its true face
It had been there all along
We chatted with it over the fencepost
Played basketball in the alley
Invited it to sit at our kitchen table
while it charmed us with stories
When the houses were known
not by the numbers, or the current
occupants, but by the surnames
of the original owners

Fear took its time
Selected its target with care
and cunning
Like a chameleon's tongue
in still frames
straight shot into the heart
of a young boy, then rolling
it back, ever so slowly
into its hunger

So slowly, there was time
for gifts and video games
and rides in the big truck
So slowly, that at first
it felt good to be eaten
So slowly, that we all wondered
how the boy could be so consumed
That somehow it was our lack
Draining innocence and replacing it
with nightmares

So slowly that even as we watched
the tongue flick and roll
we perceived nothing at all

2.

Some yahoo thought he'd do us a favor
Some yahoo thought he'd teach the perp a lesson
Some yahoo thought he was the redeemer's fire
Don't do us any more favors, yahoo
You fucked up
Fear only grew stronger
We woke up hearing it cackle
in the crackle of flame
Saw its wide orange grin filling our window
garish in the midnight
singeing our already raw nerves

Stay outta this hood, yahoo!
You only brought TV crews
sticking their microphones
into preschoolers' faces
vapid TV reporters rehearsing
their "live from the scene" lines
"Was it lightning, or something more sinister?"
Yeah, right.

What's sinister is that we have become
A nation that watches these reports
"Live, live"
Hours, days after the crime
As if that made any difference
As if the information was somehow more important
Standing in front of yellow tape or white chalk outlines
What's sinister is that people get jollies
Driving up and down the alley

Slack jawed at nothing—
a burned shell of wood
What's sinister is that no one wants to be involed
but they all line up to tell how it happended
Live
At the scene
Fear crack another beer
laughing like hell

3.

The rosebush is blooming
in spite of haphazard pruning
its nakedness through the winter
no bone meal at its feet
yet it bursts grapey corsages
on its ragly gangly stems
thorning their way sunward

The rosebush blooms
Ignoring creeping Charlie
dandilions' and daylilies' encroachment
insistent on its budding nature
against ash and soot falling
from the singed birch
It is not bothered by mothers' cries
and neighbors' talk
It does not know fear
as the boy knows fear
as his family know
as we now know

It knows water, or the lack of it
Nitrogen around its roots
Carbon dioxide leafing in the breeze
It knows this patch of clotted dirt

And earthworms' business
It is all innocent adolescence
It is going to the prom
And so unfearing, the rosebush blooms

4.

And what about the boy
Who no longer plays in the alley?
And what about the boy
Who kicks his brother's Legos?
And what about the boy
Whose smile is forced and wary?
And what about the boy
Who jackrabbits from the car to the back door?
And what about the boy
Who dreams hands and chameleon tongues?
And what about the boy?

Liberation

The cranes are free
Let loose from their cage of wood and glass
An eyelet unanchored sent them flying
In a clamor of shards and splinters

Less optimistic ornithologists
would say this is a bad omen—
on the turn of a new year
the cranes grew impatient
feeling attentions drawn away from them

"We deserve more than this shabby frame,"
they clamored to dead air,
"more than this creased and stained mat of paper"
And seeing backs turned even still
they pecked at the eyelet hole
widening it just enough . . .

The cranes perch on the dining room table
Preening, they are patient
They know we can't move without them

Theft

The fingerprint dust is everywhere
Loops and sworls in the door handles,
window moldings, the air vents
I breathe in evidence and cough it out
to the West Side whose Holy Lady of Guadalupe
blesses the wayward—the thieves or me, I wonder

Prayers were offered, and for eighty bucks
And another twenty-four for overnight storage
they were answered. My supplication
included a car wash and vacuum,
but I am chastised—the Holy Lady murmers
"You've got your wheels, now go home."

I wonder who last sat in this seat, listening
to Zone 105, cruising cyclops-eyed at night
down University, pushing the gearshift
like a dog to a washtub. Was it the leaky tire
or more flashy chrome and paint that left
my van a gawky kid on the curb
and everyone else gone to the dance?

Did the thieves think my "Teach Tolerance"
bumper sticker meant I wouldn't hold a grudge
when out running for chips and beer,

Did they drive full of braggadaccio, order a bagful
of White Castles for the driver, laughing the road
away until morning? Or did they take side streets
navigating by rearview mirror, sliding up a block
away from home, slipping like smelt through the moist dawn?

All questions of the dust I wipe away
Stories swirling, mixing with exhaust,
the breathing city,
the sighing hands of the Senora

Growing Up Indian

I remember growing up
wondering why Indians looked like me
or more like grandpa—a little in the nose
but mostly the eyes
deep and wise, tapped into knowledge
I wasn't getting at school

Even though I had a cowboy outfit
I preferred to be Cochise
when Johnny and Dale and my kid brother
played cowboys and Indians
Cochise had those eyes
And better still, he didn't play no kemosabe

When I got older and hair got longer
I thought I was Neil Young
But even guys down on Franklin
thought I was from White Earth
Maybe it was the hair, the macramé belt
fringe hanging down to my knees
swinging along to late adolescent lope

Maybe it was the way I handled the delivery van
Like it was an Appaloosa galloping down Nicollet
reining it into a turn around Loring Park
then popping the clutch so it reared up
before leaving a trail of dust, loose asphalt
and mallard dung down Hennepin
to the Greyhound Bus Depot

These days nobody much mistakes
me for Anishinable
and I don't play Cochise
But every once in a while I get a look
Like the look I must have had back then
when I wondered why Indians looked like me

Dad, Long Distance

It is not blind love
Even as she sits on his lap
asks for another story,
she knows. He has screwed up again
She knows the meaning of empty closets
The missing stereo
Doors slammed, bottles in the sink

It is why she buries
her head in his chest,
pinches his side
Why she clings like Virginia Creeper
twinned to the frayed denim of his left leg
Why she begs again
"Read more, Daddy,
Read it one more time, just once more."

Daddy has forgotten the language
Cannot translate
Hears, "more," instead of "Don't go"
Hears "again," instead of "get well"
Feels the hands clutching his jeans
But does not see the rivulets on her face
Says, "It's getting late, off to bed,"
and walks out, no longer a father

Christmas Carol

My mother bemoans the lack of song
in the oh-so-sensitive present
Children cannot sing Christmas carols in school
"It's not respectful of other cultures," they say
While grownups in flack jackets and muftis
show each other the ultimate in disrespect
for person and culture, ignoring history

My mother was raised Buddhist
but remembers how she sang
with no less glee than her classmates
Christmas carols in the third grade
Extra-special because it was her first time
singing four-part harmony—
the alto counterpoint to the soprano descant
still fresh and clear as December air

My mother later walking in the church aisle
with the same fervor singing
as she does today, this daughter
of a Japanese tenant farmer joining
her voice with a ninety-three-year-old
descendant of Bonnie Prince Charlie's
flight from Scotland,

as if it was the third-grade class
nothing more than that
two voices singing in Latin
"Adeste Fidelis"

Restless

So close to All Souls' Day
when the wall between now and evermore
is thin and more permeable,
Pearl is agitated
walks through my dreaming

How could it be?
Just before her birthday
This mean-spirited, selfish man
who does not understand the world
outside of his walls and walls and walls
Who would
Keep out
Put down
Send back
Reverse the flow of history
Is now the president-elect
Of the country Pearl had worked to
make a place of bridge-builders—
Caretakers of the infrastucture
that knits us all as humans?

She paces a ghostly frown
What to do? What to do?
I call to her, "Remember yourself
Calm and rational
You, who even still
pull out the best of human nature."

And so we plot
How to infiltrate the Oval Office
And infuse it with her spirit
The White House haunted
Not with fear and division
But with a vision of open arms
And open minds
All walls tumbling, tumbling
down

OBITUARIES
LEVERTOV, Denise. 10/24/1928–12/20/1997_____

Elegy

How I could have missed Denise Levertov's
passage to air, I do not know
Perhaps it was my own zigzag path
retracing dead ends to dead ends
finally noticing a pattern and following
a different course so that even her words
so deft and full of purpose, got tangled
and did not reach my ears
Thoughts turned inward, wires crossed
Sparking, but producing no current

So, three years passing I find delight and sorrow
This Great Unknowing, her final guidebook
though I think mistitled, for she knew well
the spirit worlds, the place of dreams
and its inhabitants—unbidden bringers
of the word, inspiration

Her wisdom flashes even as the flash of splitting atoms
imbedded a human imprint on the witnessing bank wall,
imprinted themselves in my flesh
altering thoughts, perceptions, structures
A self-perpetuating reaction
changing life to spirit, atoms to energy
This fire of creation
A fusion reaction, not of hydrogen, but words

OBITUARIES
GRUCHOW, Paul. 5/23/1947–2/22/2004_____

Where You Will Find Him

If you are looking for Paul, you will not find him here
Oh, yes, you will recognize a semblance
of him in each other's eyes, the aura
that rubbed off on us all as he talked
His words seeping through skin,
pulsing through our bodies
Changing the way we think
The way we look out at the world

But if you really want to discourse
with the man,
this is not the place
Not confined within walls
Nor walking the floors of long-dead oaks

Go find a plot of prairie
Walk until you bare deep into big bluestem,
Blue-eyed grass, and ghostly white larkspur
Find the clump of western prairie fringed orchid
and wait
Wait for the bobolink to bob and weave
along the swelling seed heads
It will land behind you, but do not turn
Not yet
Wait until it calls to you, then turn
Look it in the eye
See the twinkling you remember
And listen
Deeply listen

OBITUARIES
FELDMAN, Bob. xx/xx/1949–1/11/2006_____

How Our Yellow and Blue House
Became a Red House
Beneath the Paint

He came to the house just once
but it was enough
to saturate the walls
with mirth and music
His history along with the melody
Of letting the musicians make the music
while he ran the business,
is there whenever whirling dimples of metal
contact light, become sound
Not his magic, but his pleasure
Pleasing us that celebratory evening
turning white wine into Champagne
after black beans and rice, poached salmon
Singing Bobby Dylan, old Irish airs
and Warren Zevon, no howlin'
wolf more throaty than his own
So that now, with his falling away
the walls shift and the notes change—
the thirds and sevenths flattened,
less lilty. But still,
if you put your palms flat
on paint and old plaster,
a vibration—soft, unmistakable
His chuckle, his gift
of sound and song

BOURASSA, Marguerite Isabel (née Chisholm). 2/20/1913–1/24/2011_____

Singing Partner

Who will be my singing partner?
Remembering the verses
to the old Scots and Irish ballads
Singing with gusto
Bonnie Prince Charlie's
flight from Culloden's fields,
or the young maid rejecting
a marriage of money
to follow her heart with an outlaw
across the border,
or drinking one more draught
with comrades on a moonlit night . . ..
The songs our bond of love
But only the surface
of what you have taught me
Your spirit and wisdom the best regifting
Our shared songs and stories rippling outwards
Speed bonnie boat like a bird on the wing
Onward! The sailors cry
Carry dear Margo, who is our true queen
Over the sea to Skye

Loch Lomond Revisited

Margo has always taken the high road
In deed and in spirit
Though the songs says
the low road is the quicker path
back to Scotland
It seems too ponderous
for our Margo
even in death, she takes not the low road
nor the high road
but the higher road
of falcons and angels

So we'll take the high road
and she'll take the higher road
And Margo's in Scotland already
For me and my song mate
Shall never meet again
On the bonnie banks of Superior

Obituaries
Angelou, Maya (née Marguerite Annie Johnson). 4/4/1928–5/28/2014____

The Singing Bird

The singing bird has flown
But has left her voice
It reverberates the cadence
of a president addressing the poor
the underserved
as citizens, a very real demographic
It sings with the throngs
of men and women
able to marry the one they love
It warbles a lullaby of hope
to calm a new generation
to inspire them
yes, there are matters worth fighting for
It cries a warning
That the blood of history
is still on our streets
That civil rights
are neither yet civil
nor equal rights for all

Not yet
But look
The cage door is open
It begs a response
Let her voice fill our souls
with purpose
that we too, abandon
our cages
to fly

OBITUARIES
DALY, Sean Francis. 2/18/1964–12/17/2014_____

December 17, 2014

The morning light white off the lake
Off the snow and birches
Like Sean's soul
finally free from
the fragile crust
of a body
that alcohol turned
into a prison

Yesterday, confined
to a hospice bed,
see how he moves now!
Like a winger
on a break-away
Fluid as he never was
even at his best—
a dip of the shoulder
a flick of the wrist
Sean makes his goal
at last

Playing It Out

Sean has his mother's sense of timing
An actor, choosing his moment
and owning it

So now
On the same day
Nearly the same hour
The uncle he tended with love
and vigilance
through the last days,
chose to leave
Sean reaches out,
grabs Jack's hand
as he passes in his yearly cycle
becoming like Gemini
two linked souls
now in the sky
Renegades
Misfits, big of heart
Making mischief in the heavens

OBITUARIES
KUSUNOKI, Pearl Misayo (née Fujimoto). 11/10/1929–2/13/2015_____

Pearl, the Poet

My mother was a poet
though she would say
she did not write poems
Pearl looked well at the world
and interpreted its beauty
Transforming a person
sculpting hair
metaphor for a new image
Envisioning a garden
with bulbs and seeds
her lines and stanzas
Transforming the blooms
into another art form
Arranging them into living
creatures of petal and foliage

My mother was a poet
though folks would say
in her deeds
reconciling the darkness
with her light touch
a meal
a word
transforming strangers and friends
wherever she was
at the Red Cross
at church
at the hospital
How she brought people together
Forgiving even the government camps
that stole her adolescence

My mother was a poet
though she would say
she did not write poems
But, oh, her words!
The thank you letters
that recipients would save
because of the beauty of her script
and the profundity of the content
Her impromptu graces
at family meals and holidays
celebrating and magnifying
our own bits of life
taking on even the minister's mantle
in prayer

My mother was a poet
even at the end
frustrated that the words she loved
would not materialize
no matter how hard she struggled
to shape them into air
Reduced to head nods
and squeezing hands,
she managed two words
distinct and clear:

When the hospital chaplain
read the words of Rumi, "Beautiful."
And then the words of Mary Oliver, "Beautiful."
And finally, near midnight
when it was time to take Dad
home to rest,
her benediction to us all
simple, yet carrying an ocean of meaning,
"Bye."

Bye

After all the words you said
Well-chosen
Precise and distinctive
Some might find it ironic
Your last utterance
So simple and plain

But think the way you saw it
in your perfect schoolgirl script—
the looping upward of the b
the tiniest of smiles
linking the b to the y
the downwards ellipse below the line
ending with the unpretentious
curve of the e

And of course
you in your poet's heart
knowing it is not finality
but transitional
Goodbye
"God be with ye
Until we meet again"

Bye, Mom, Bye

Pearl's Not Done Yet

And didn't she bring us all together
And doesn't she challenge us all
to play her life forward
looking for the humanity
In every face?

And doesn't she open new eyes to poetry
and art?
The beauty in the simple miracles:
Mary Oliver's grasshopper,
the opening of chrysalises

And doesn't she open ears to music?
Different cultures
singing together
the same song
in a tongue not their own

And doesn't she teach us to pray
with humility
Blessing the other
instead of drawing attention to the self

And doesn't she teach us
Her work is not done
if someone is mistreated
left alone
homeless or hungry
while we squander
the riches around us

And doesn't she remind us
in the rains of spring
the sprouting slivers of daffodil
the unfolding of clematis
the sparrows' chatter
the cardinals' whistle
to have big hearts
and open minds
To truly live in this
gift of a world

Late Night, Driving Home from
St. Cloud

"Look up here, I'm in heaven,"
sings David Bowie
Not going softly into his
Good night
Percussive much of the time
Driving beats propel the darkness
Saxophone his preferred solo voice
This time, crooning, keening, wailing
the night highway
A challenging listen
Yet moments of tenderness
David unfettered leaves a sonic legacy

"Look up here, I'm in danger,"
As if he wasn't dangerous enough
Life on the edge
Chameleon, not content
With done that
Being instead where no one
has been
all to melodious hooks
and dancey beats
All the more safe
To challenge the norms
Be who you thought you could not
Be—especially at school
At work, in front of the 'rents

What more to give
When you've given all you had?
A map to the unexpected
A safe house for the different ones
And music
Edgy, bouncy, jazzy
Suave and rough music
to juxtapose our own lyrics over
Both yin and yang
Our bright and dark star

4/21/16

There is a hole in the sky
over Minnesota
And wherever we look
It seems all we see is purple

But look closer
They say a rainbow
Appeared over Paisley Park
It is all of us
multi-colored
riding the arc of ultra violet
Crossing genres
Crossing cultures
Crossing forms, taboos
Confounding those
who thought music and art
must be pigeon-holed
to be marketed and appreciated

You flipped the bird
At those corregated minds
with an unpronounceable symbol
jumped the big boat
when it could no longer hold
the breadth and depth
of your expression

So that we who trail
your oceans-wide wake
have more freedom
just to be ourselves—
the rainbow

And though the rain is falling
we are dancing like crazy
with you, filling
the hole in the sky

OBITUARIES
COHEN,Leonard.9/21/1934–11/7/2016_____

Hallelujah

While it could be said that Dylan was the voice of the generation
it was Joni Mitchel and you who were our lives' muses
The ins and outs of relationships, worries and foibles
and an understanding of the light and the dark . . .

Was it the new darkness, so universal and opaque
that you felt your light could no longer illuminate?
Was it the bigotry and hate that did you in
your poet's soul recalling showers of poison gas
and the firey furnace?

Whatever it was, it was almost like the blues
minor fourth and seventh on the fifth
seemingly simple repetitive figures
so complex in nuance, the things left out
that drew us into the world we knew
but had no words for

Leaving us with new visions
The tryst between fire and Joan
Marianne and Alexandra both leaving
Suzanne and the Sisters of Mercy
all populate the life just behind the veil
the life you knew so well, and now yourself
a denzien and legend
Hallelujah!

Section C:

Weather, Outdoors, and Personals

Snowmaker

I now understand
My blooming forsythia makes the snow fall
The first year,
I thought it was a fluke, bad luck
An evil witch's curse
Sunny stars, but frosted hood
weighing heavy on their heads

But now, three years running
With careful scientific observation
I have watched the budding
progress of the bush

The weather warms
The weather chills
The sky leadens and leavens
But nothing happens—Nothing

Nothing for days until
The optimistic forsythia wakes
blinks its myriad starry eyelids
do the flakes begin to fall

She Said, "It's Not a Spring Sky."

It's a fall sky
Sad and beautiful
like something's leaving
Light angular under steel-wool clouds
Even the trees unbudded
embarrassed to be naked so late in the season

We wonder if spring itself
Has left us behind
The Doppler effect, train-whistle wind
through bare branches,
the fields we drive by still unplanted
the farmer's sorrow, a lover's quarrel with the weather

I turn off the radio
And we drive in silence
A thin line of gravel dust
follows us, a wake
for a season that never happened

At the Cabin

The clouds here do not have silver linings
They are dreamsicles, all orange and golden at the edges
And creamy where the frame meets the slatey silhouette
It is ludicrous stocking the minivan to capacity
with groceries, luggage, and booze
to come here and rough it,
but the dreamsicle light forgives human foolishness
blesses us with the perfect reflecting moment
where the life outside is on standby

Claudia remarks how thoughtful the trees are
to have framed the lake for our pleasure
How they define this piece of earth
The blue of the sky, the blue of the lake
with a green sliver in between—our domain
I walk the sliver in silence
Indian paintbrush, ferns nodding, wild iris
step with me, wary of two-legged intruders
They know the sound of chainsaws
the foreboding knocking of hammer to nail

Tenacity

Oh, how life holds on to itself!
Look, the over-wintered impatiens
reduced to broken stems
Yet at its base
and at each stem joint
a new leaf stretches upward

And the azalea
Dead to the world
while its two sisters blossomed
full of their finery
now pushing out first growth
on its own calendar

Blessings then, on late bloomers
and those who wait
instead of uprooting and planting
this year's replacements

Blessings on the nurturing soil
and the persistent rain
and the gardener's hope

Blessings on atoms of carbon and oxygen
fused and unfused
through photosynthesis
and the grand designer
who set all this tenacity
in motion

The Solstice Moon

They told us it would be the largest moon in 167 years
This lining up of solstice, perigee
Celestial serendipity
"We could drive at night without headlights!"
some exclaimed,
while others, stuffy,
"You won't be able to tell
any difference."
The moon doesn't care
Doesn't rely on the *Farmer's Almanac*
Nor the calculations of astronomers and physicists

It is the wolves howling, the chiming of ice crystals
in the northern sky
It is blue-shadowed wonder in a four-year-old's eyes
It is flying reindeer and oil lamps that do not run dry
It is the full bounty of the year past
It is the messenger of the year to come

The moon pulls upward
Our feet stuck in the earth, rending topsoil,
resurrecting what was before
the sun's ascendency—
The mysteries of reflected light
Whole and not whole
Eaten by darkness and rebirthing
The measure of time

The moon does not care about percentages
Scoffs at publicity, the paparazzi
Resumes its nightly walk
Smiles at itself in upturned gawky faces,
The pacing wolves
The Druids' whispers
The hushing snow

The Last Dance of the Crab Apple Tree

The crab apple tree was resplendent
in its floral gown
while others, barely a leaf to cover
their winter nakedness
The crab apple tree basked in compliments
from Nike sweat joggers,
in turned heads and jealous looks

The crab apple tree tossed her crown
and danced above the garden
Laughing at pale green shoots
Her ruffling voice saying,
"You poor things, you will never
Be as magnificent
as stunning
as graceful as me"

Laughing and dancing
even as the sky turned to slate
and sparrows skittered deep into the blue spruce
Laughing and dancing
until the machete wind cut her at the ankles
dashing her head against the neighboring linden

Leaving a hole
A vacant spotlight dance
Where creeping Charlie and crabgrass now thrive

The Nursing Log

I will sit here and eat the dirt of centuries
rings of wood fiber broken down
feeding on histories, now carbon and oxygen,
hydrogen and nitrogen,
each element releasing voices
a song with no sequence it seems
but listen! A massed choir so complex
I cannot give it my own voice
though it sounds into my marrow
Resonating deeper still
as my roots crack the fiber of this nursing log
Voice, breath in anticipation
Some day when I break the crown
of this redwood grove
I will join in the song of songs
to life universal

_____

What Do My Hands Do . . .

. . . when you're not here?
How can they steal sections of the morning paper,
serve coffee in bed?
They reach out to be kissed,
Rough up your hair
Feel only dead air
Impatient, they do dishes
only to find no hands
waiting with the drying towel
They pour a drink,
but toast only emptiness

Nighttime's the worst
Where do they go?
They search for the warm curve of your hip,
and finding only sheet,
they scrunch under the pillows
Pouting
Until they are rudely tingled
awake by nerves demanding
blood and oxygen

They try to sleep on my belly—
A poor substitute
They are not fooled
Tossing and turning
Exhausted finally
sulking into slumber
dreaming of roundness
They wake in the morning cupped
Waiting to receive you home

Yearbook

I looked you up in the high school yearbook
Out of curiosity
Just to see maybe
We could have hung out
Back in those days
Of sit-ins
The entire world, it seemed
Going through changes

And there you were
The seventh row of photos
Page 200, Junior class
And I knew why we didn't cross paths
My dork shoegazer
Would not know what to say
And you would find me frustratingly uncommunicative
Or intriguingly mysterious
But not the stuff that makes friends
Not then

So here we are now so many years later
With this new information
And another transition for you
"Retire" meaning putting on new and different treads
Spinning off down a freshly-paved road
And me again in the dust
But this time perhaps
A new-found connection
Impossible in high school
Fostered by the give and take of a decade
Just might
Take root and grow

Kid Sister

You were always Tim's kid sister
The girl across the street, not quite privy
to our dogpack, but close enough
to ride your brother's outgrown Stingray
while we rode our five-speeds
up and down the dirt pile, raced laps around the church

Later, when summers opened garage doors
And Tim and Paul and Greg and me played "Louie, Louie"
Or "House of the Rising Sun," you were there on the edges
because you were the sister, and it was your garage, too

When the band stopped and the record player played slow songs
the girls my age, Jackie and Diane and Mary, would hang
around your drummer brother, and Paul and Greg, quick on the uptake
would grab the ones left in the garage semi-darkness
when Tim took a turn on the dance floor or slipped out
behind the lilac bushes, leaving you and me
to stand awkwardly or dance

I still feel how you fit—how you almost
had to get up on tip-toe to rest your head
on my shoulder, the giddiness of your breasts
pressed against me murmuring
How I held you after the song stopped
To feel just one or two more heartbeats passing
between your white cotton blouse and my gym shirt
before the fast songs started again

And after that, stopping by your house was not so much to see Tim
Though we still jammed in the basement, I hung out after
the other guys left, and your mom, all-knowing offered 7-Up
and invited me to dinner while we pretended to be fascinated
by family photo albums, or something you knitted all by yourself—
something in your room, and wouldn't I like to see it?

And you mom calling "dinner" after modest minutes passed
The steaming bowl of spaghetti in the middle of the table
with extra sauce—a discovery savored twice by remembering:
Mom spaghetti is comfort, but someone else's mom's spaghetti
is exotic. And milk in green Texan plastic tumblers
is never as cool and sweet as it is when ankle
brushes friend's kid sister's feet beneath the kitchen table

Partners
(for J.S.)

Three years in your realm of teaching
is yesterday's lesson plan
but for me, it is half the life I have lived as a teacher
What greater Masters course than to work with you
Share adventures and mistakes
Boggle students with problems
Only to have them boggle us back
Real-life math, the best kind

But more than numbers, this partnership
Solid footing in times of doubt
A good ear for complaints and frustrations
A firm, sisterly nudge when diabetes hit
And the reinforcing high five
when the blood counts came back good
Add politics and music, our undercurrent
Real-life studies, the best kind

So now I am a thief burying inside the teacher brain
your bits of treasure to pass on and on
to Rishabh and Joey and Ariel and Jennifer
All who continue to thrive from your gift
And all who will now get it second-hand from me
Real-life teaching, the best kind

Slam Granny
(for C.H.)

In the beginning was the word
And the word became Slam Granny
And Slam Granny took herself to the 'hoods
And the 'hoods responded
Words upon words
being fruitful and multiplying

Words from the southside
From the northside high schools
to downtown juvi-detention
to the Slam Nationals
and cornershop coffeehouses

The words came back
And turned heads
And changed lives
In turn, changing this here
Community

"T'aint nothin'," says Slam Granny,
"to do with li'l ol' me.
All those scribes and poets and hip-hoppers
Doin' it,"
she says, trying as always
to avoid the spotlight
Too late, Slam Granny!
The words came back to us
And we know who was the mother
And midwife, and the holy spirit
of word
don't be shucking us now, Slam Granny
just let all the words
come gather 'round you
and give you thanks

White Boy
(for D.M)

Growing up I was a white boy
Not the person I grew into
This person the students assume
is Hmong, with the still-not-quite-right eyes
and nose somewhere between Lakota and Ojibway

No, no
When I was growing up, I had sandy hair
and freckles, and I liked baseball
even though I struck out at T-ball
I got Harmon Killebrew's autograph
and loved the impossible, unattainable
golden Heiki, or tomboy Janet,
or shy Theresa, my first kiss,
not the Japanese girls who giggled
when my parents tried to make introduction
during sukiyaki dinners at my grandparents'
musty church Nordeast

When I was growing up, I was a white boy
who didn't eat foreign food
except when we went to the Tokyo Café
and even there, I ate curry chicken
that was stolen in the old country from English sailors
Of course there was New Year's Day
And all the food that Mom and Grandma
And all the relatives in the area made:
Teriyaki, makisushi, shrimp tempura
and jiggly slippery konten,
but not one hot dog in sight

When I was growing up, I was a white boy
I was Johnny Quest and Napoleon Solo
I was Space Angel and Paladin
And the Chuck Connors dude
With the rifle you could shoot with one hand
I was not King Fu cricket
Not Momotaro, the peach boy
Not shogun, not even samurai
Maybe Cochise once in a while
But that was it with ethnic acting

When I was growing up I was a white boy
White as my name, taken from English explorer
Colonizer for the queen
I was not Kusunoki, but Kusi, the coos
"hey Kusi,"—a handle just like the jocks
I got Adidas when they first came out, and Frye boots
I did not sing "Sukiyaki," no, it was "Suite Judy Blue Eyes"
Aspiring to fringed-leather Neil Young hairdo

So why the change?
Trauma, bad Karma
A dream inherited
Of dust and barbed wire
The steely glint of desert sun
from the watchtower man's binoculars

Maybe it was my parents' youth interrupted
The long outhouse lines
The Poston dust
Or Topaz winter stretching like iced fences
across the desert
Maybe it was Aunt Bessie's tuberculosis
Yozi's asthma, Grandma's comma posture
Something pulled back the gauzy chrysalis

to free some crazy mix of warrior butterfly
armed with the anger of too much quiet, too long
tempered by words, words, words
and a kick in the butt from a brother
cut from the same kimono cloth

But when I was growing up, I was a white boy

Times Two

The times turn on us
The times twine us
All the years and tears
And grand guffaws
Knitting with the patience of Kronos
Our lives
So when we step back
The fabric
Two fibers
Complimentary colors
Become one piece
Rainbow strong
Our own silk

ACKNOWLEDGEMENTS

"The 49 Bus . . ." first appeared in *Drumvoices Review*, Southern Illinois University at Edwardsville.

"Airport" and "Items in the News" appeared as earlier versions in *Cool Hearts*, TCFN/SASE Writers Conference.

"The Shadowgraph Speaks" appeared in *Rochester (MN) Magazine* and was performed at the Rochester Peace Walk and Rally.

"Growing Up Indian" appeared in *The Definitive Guide to the Twin Cities*, Spout Press, and was part of the performance piece *Landbridge: The Beringia Project*, written and performed by Stan Kusunoki and Jamison Mahto at Intermedia Arts with support from The Minnesota State Arts Board "Cultural Collaborations" Grant, and the Jerome Foundation.

Thanks to Corinne, Curtis, and Anne at North Star Press for their energy and devotion. Special thanks to Claudia Daly, editor nonpareil, muse, cheerleader, and also my wife. Thanks again to my standby support group: Carolyn Holbrook, Mary Jo Thompson, John Coy, David Mura, Mankwe Ndosi, Lia Rivamonte, Evelina Chao, Joe Kadi, Margaret Hasse, John Minczeski, and Diego Vasquez Jr.; and newfound pals, Kathryn Kyser, Hawona Sullivan Janzen, Michael Kleber-Diggs, and Sagirah Shahib.

Thanks to all independent bookstores, but especially to Subtext, and David Unowsky (St. Paul), Lake Country Booksellers (White Bear Lake), The Bookstore at Fitgers (Duluth), Eat My Words (Minneapolis), and to the Shakopee Public Library.

Thanks also to Janet Waller and Barnes & Noble HarMar Mall in Roseville.

CPSIA information can be obtained
at www.ICGtesting.com
Printed in the USA
LVOW03s0335150817

545026LV00007B/8/P